To Glaro?

Enjoy
poetry ale
brother's &
the wonderful items
by my sister great niece
This truly is a family pa'g

Jayne
Randall

MW01614133

Reflections of a Mother, The Poetry Of Marjorie K. Randall

Additional Poetry From
Steven Randall
and
Jayne Randall

Produced and Edited By
Jayne Randall

Illustrations By
Beverly Detroy
and
Kristina Gil

Marjorie K. Randall
1922 - 2005

*Her children will arise up,
and call her blessed*

Proverbs 31:28a

Introduction

This is a compilation of the poetry of
Marjorie K. Randall, known as Marge to
everyone, and the mother of eight children.
When she passed away, she also had fifteen
grandchildren, and four great-
grandchildren, and her life was filled with
her family. And, yet throughout the years,
she made time to record her thoughts and
feelings in her poetry.

Marge's poetry encompasses so many aspects
of life and death, but mainly her reflections
on her family. Although her marriage to
Buck (Verlin, Sr.) ended in divorce after 36
years of marriage, the legacy of the family
lives on. Her children, John, Lin (Verlin, Jr.),
Beverly, Buzz (Gregory), Jaynie (Jayne),
Barb (Barbara), Wally (Walter), and Steve,
and their children were her main
inspiration. Her brother and sisters, "Uncle"
Johnny, "Aunt" Jaynie, and "Aunt" Barbie,
and their families also inspired her poetry.
But she was also inspired by the antics of a
robin, the thought of how a dewdrop is
formed, as well as her thoughts on a kitchen,
a sonic boom, and where a star really is.

Although a poem should be able to stand
alone with no further explanation, when we
add the inspiration for a poem it gains a
depth of emotion that enhances the poem.
Unless otherwise noted, the descriptions of
the inspirations were penned by Marge.

Introduction

Beverly inherited Marge's artistic ability, and she has drawn most of the illustrations for this compilation. Marge's great-granddaughter Kristina also inherited artistic ability and has also provided some illustrations.

Originally, we compiled Marge's poetry as a Christmas gift to the family in 1997. Typical of Marge, even her cover note to the family was a poem. We hope you enjoy it as much as we have!

Jayne Randall
(Jaynie)

Reflections of a Mother,
The Poetry Of
Marjorie K. Randall

The Randall Family circa 1972.
Seated: Barbara, Beverly, and Wally.
Kneeling: Jayne and Steve.
Standing: Buzz, Marge, Buck, John, and Lin.

Christmas, 1997

Dear Family and Friends,

This is simply a rhyming journal
Of my thoughts, mostly maternal,
That my dear Jaynie has compiled
In a, perhaps, undeserved style
Which gives them more beauty and a
glamorous look
Than my starkly plain old tattered notebook.
But, for the words, you all have
a generous share
Of credit for they're the history of events
beyond compare.
Memories, moods, moments in time
That dance in my head 'til I put
them in rhyme.

All my love,
Mom (Marjorie K. Randall)

P.S. Again, I thank Jaynie
For this lovely rendition
Of my thoughts and love -
Our own Special Edition!

3

Inspiration For
To Begin - I Saw A Robin

*I'm often very happy in my own little
world. I'm just not disciplined enough
to catch the words as they dance by.*

To Begin - I Saw A Robin

By Marjorie K. Randall
May 5, 1961

My life has not been wasted
For, this morning, I composed
A beautiful, beautiful picture
Painted all in prose.

Words raced, madly, thru' my brain -
I just had to take my pen
And record my word painting;
My inspired, artistic yen.

To begin - I saw a robin,
And noticed patches of green
New buds peeking out on branches,
And the sunshine was supreme!

What words did my mind utter,
Describing these signs of spring?
Let us see - could I forget
So soon - sun - trees - robin sings?

Now the world will never know
My talents, for, in my haste
To find my pen and paper,
My ideas went to waste!

Inspiration For
Elusive, Elusive Lisa

Lin's daughter, Lisa!

*Of course, this is about my first
granddaughter who has always made me
happier just to see her.*

*Now she brings her children when she comes,
and I love them all,
Jason, Sean, Samantha, and Kristina, and
their father, Tim Blackaby!*

Elusive, Elusive Lisa

By Marjorie K. Randall
June 18, 1969

Elusive, elusive Lisa -
Willow-O-the-Wisp at play -
Darting through her childhood -
Even her shadow is gay!

It "scrunches" down to hide from danger -
It's tall when she reaches for treasures
It has a tight grip on her footsteps -
But dances its own way in pleasure.

Like elusive, elusive Lisa -
Her shadow is ruled by the sun -
Always around when the light is bright –
And curled up to sleep when
                the night time comes.

Inspiration For
If My Eyes Have Matured

One day I noticed a robin trying to fly off
with a tangled kite-string that was hanging
from our fence.

It would fly as far as it could when the
string would stop its flight and then it would
go back and start all over.

Steve went out and cut the string into
shorter lengths and hung them on the fence.

The robin came back and was so happy that
it gathered every piece in its beak,
and it flew back to its nest
looking like it was carrying a bowl of
spaghetti!

If My Eyes Have Matured

By Marjorie K. Randall

It's been a long, long time,
As an adult, I have found,
Since I have grown up
And moved away from the ground.
It seems like forever
Since my eyes could glean
Little bits of adventure
From Nature's every day scene -
Fireflies sleeping under leaves,
A caterpillar inching along,
Birds building nests of bits
Salvaged with labor and song.
Nor have I opened a pod,
To release the milkweed's seed,
Or puffed my cheeks to blow
A ripe dandelion to the breeze;
Or dammed up a ditch,
Or peeled back a sapling's bark,
Or snapped off a crisp leaf,
Or studied my pet's paw marks.
If my eyes have matured, along with
the rest of me,
Tell me - where have they gone-
The everyday wonders I used to see?

Inspiration For
"Piggy's" And "Woo's" Roaming Yen

These pigs were not my favorite pets. We had a "mini" farm and the pigs and chickens were a lot of work.

But "Barneyview" was my favorite home, and Johnny was certainly my favorite brother!

Comment from Jayne: This poem was written when Marge was 16 years old which is why it carries her maiden name.

"Piggy's" And "Woo's" Roaming Yen

By Marjorie K. Shuman

1938

I locked one in the chicken coop
And chased out all the chickens
I raced the other thru' the field -
We ran just like the dickens!
He headed for his little home,
But was afraid to enter.
I coaxed and coaxed, but to no avail -
The fence was torn in the center.
I put some feed on the other side
And waited until he was half thru' it -
I jumped behind and began to shove,
But, alas, I just couldn't do it.
I yelled for help and Johnny came -
Piggy and I were near tears.
After a long and difficult chase -
I had its tail and Johnny its ears.
Piggy squealed and fought us both,
But we hung on with all our might -
We shoved him back thru' the fence -
We'd won, but were we a sight!!! (Phew!)
Now to get the other pig -
We ran back to the coop -
Unlocked the door and got a rope
And made a lasso loop.
I chased the pig -
Boy - did she squeal!
We ran past John
And he roped her heel.

continued..

"Piggy's" And "Woo's" Roaming Yen
(continued)

Now the pigs live peacefully
In their homey little pen.
They've promised faithfully to warn us
When they get the roaming yen.

Inspiration For
The Public Demands

This is a little bit "dated," but this was based on 1960's commercials. But - on the other hand - has anything really changed?

B Detray 2016

The Public Demands

By Marjorie K. Randall
October 27, 1960

If soap that doesn't bubble
Gets clothes the snowiest white -
If shaving underwater,
Makes men a handsome sight -
If pens that write on butter
Bring about an intellectual Golden Age
When machines answer every question
And microfilm saves every printed page -
If infra-rays replace cooking dinner
And pills put you to sleep - or keep you
awake -
If man-made furs are better than Nature's -
And aerosol sprays conceal the world's
mistakes-
If every task is done in an instant,
And jets whisk you from here to there -
Why must an up-to-date lady
Still suffer a tortuous diet,
harness her fat in girdles,
camouflage her complexion,
dye her hair?
In this day of modern wonders
The Female Public should really clamor
For a concentrated improvement -
A pill for Instant Glamour!

Inspiration For
"Contagious"

Wally and Steve must have had the
Measles in '61. That makes this
an "historical" poem.

"Contagious"

By Marjorie K. Randall
April 24, 1961

Where do Measles go when they disappear
From a pink, polka-dotted little boy's nose?
Do they just drop off in heaps upon the floor-
Discarded, like laundry, as he sheds his
clothes?

Were they painted by a "Measle Artist"?
Whose mission in life, he must think,
Is to find fresh scrubbed Boy and Girl faces
To splatter with splotches of riotous pink!

Inspiration For
Where Is A Star?

I've always wondered, "If the stars, etc. all
have different orbits, and the scientists and
astronomers are correct about the speed of
light - wouldn't we be seeing the same stars
more than once at the same time?"

Oh well - now you know
how my brain works - such as it is!

Where Is A Star?

By Marjorie K. Randall

If the stars in the sky are
Millions of Light Years away,
How can we ever really know
Where to find each star today?
Stars we see aren't even there -
We only know they passed
Through our heavens years ago,
Leaving trails like sparkling glass
Which glitter like diamonds,
But must be more transparent,
For we just see what isn't there -
And trust that this is where it went!

Inspiration For
Truck Stop

Long car trips with the family were always an adventure!

Buck would always say, "We'll stop at the next one," but the "next one" was always closed. When we finally found one that suited him, out in the "hinter" lands - the food would always taste like kerosene, etc.!

Truck Stop

By Marjorie K. Randall
July, 1961

A sign pulsating
Throughout the black night
Beckons tired drivers
To stop for a bite.

It blinks on and off
Tho' no one can see -
It works all night long
For strangers like me.

This light earns no pay -
The spectator's joy
Sighting its welcome
Justifies its employ.

Inspiration For
Child's Eye View

It isn't easy being a parent. You are responsible for keeping children clean, healthy, suitably dressed, educated, loved, but not overly indulgent, etc., etc., etc.

Just don't think I didn't realize your "side" of the situation, too!

Child's Eye View

By Marjorie K. Randall
October, 1970

Hordes of grown-ups
Are closing in on me,
Mouthing their ideas
Of how my life should be;
Deciding when my eyes should open -
And, when they should go to sleep -
What, and when to feed my body,
So, in their image I will keep
A clean and healthy childhood,
Developing, at the "Proper" Pace
Until they decide that I've grown-up
And can fly to outer space.

Inspiration For
Sonic Boom - Boom - Boom

*I loved living beside the airport! Especially
when our 12 dogs and cats sat, side-by-side,
and watched you kids play ball –
or just watched the planes land!*

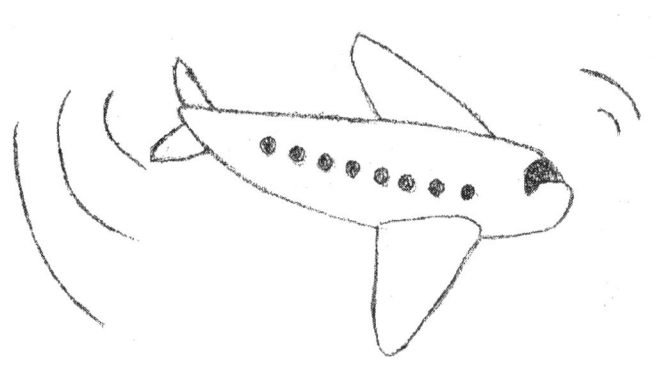

Sonic Boom - Boom - Boom

By Marjorie K. Randall

1970

Supersonic planes
Originate that boom
High up in the air
And it trails them
Along the ground
Following everywhere -
Shaking windows,
Cracking plaster -
Speed is progress
But noise is Master!

Inspiration For
Just One Ordinary Boy

This was about Steve, as he was our last little boy, but it could have been about all of my little boys.

B Delroy 2016

Just One Ordinary Boy
By Marjorie K. Randall

How does Santa Claus know
    if I was good or bad this year?
I'm sure such a popular gentleman as he
Is too busy to peek or try to overhear
Just one little ordinary fella like me.

Gee, Santa, next year I'll really, really be
    good -
If, tonight, you will close your eyes and
    overlook
The many times, this year, I was in a bad
    mood,
And pick my Christmas Toys
    from the Good things in your book!

Inspiration For
Hair Despair

The boys always let their hair grow longer during vacation from school.

Buck would get upset over it, and I'd tell him not to worry as I knew they'd get it cut when they went back to school sports.

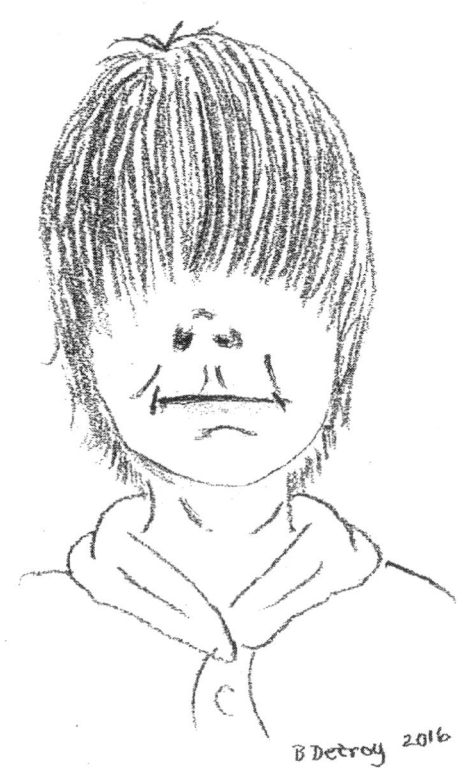

B Detroy 2016

Hair Despair

By Marjorie K. Randall
July 8, 1970

We couldn't communicate
About the length of the hair -
We tried to understand
And did our best not to stare -
But it began to curl and spill
Around the shoulders and eyes,
And we averted our gaze
And sent silent prayers to the skies.
The answer came this week-end,
Without a word of reproach -
The boys all went to the barber -
Just to please the coach!

Inspiration For
A Fragile Wisp Of A Lady
(Mrs. McGee)

*This is about Lonnie Kline's Grandmother.
I'm glad that, the last time I saw her, she was
standing in her front yard - no lawn, but
millions of flowers (many taller than she) -
straw hat with a floppy large brim with a
gentle breeze blowing wisps of the
purist white hair about her face. It was
enough to "paint" a picture in my mind
that I'll never forget.*

A Fragile Wisp Of A Lady
(Mrs. McGee)

By Marjorie K. Randall

A fragile wisp of a lady -
Ethereal as finest lace,
Gentle of voice and manner,
Beautiful of thought and face.
Strength, unsurpassed in time of need,
Suffering, defeated with prayer,
Experience, worn proudly as beads,
Collects love as though it was rare.

What keeps this life, this gentle breeze
That barely ruffles the world's leaves,
That causes no storms, or asks no favors,
That lives as calmly as it breathes?
Long ready to face her Maker,
Yet, lives past younger generations -
This fragile wisp of a lady
Is God-chosen, deserving veneration.

31

Inspiration For
Winter Burial

Aunt Barbie's infant son, Monte.

In memory of Monte Noel Richards who was taken by Sudden Infant Death Syndrome at 6 weeks of age.

Winter Burial

By Marjorie K. Randall

So quick - so quick -
Oh, where did your breath of life go?
So brief - so brief -
But, not too brief to hold all my love,
Yesterdays - so happy with
　　　　　the creation of you,
My baby - my baby,
The fulfillment of my life,
Not empty evermore
For I held you close to me -
Felt your heart beat - your fingers grasp -
Nourished you - nourished you,
One moment so full of life!
How could it happen?　Did I let you go?
I lost you - I lost you -
But I'll never lose you!
You are here - Why are you here
In this tiny jewel box on the snow?

Inspiration For
Doyle's Tree

I think that this is one of my favorite poems. It was about the tree beside our house on the farm in Lexington, Indiana.

I think it was an Elm tree. It always kept its leaves until spring, and suddenly, one beautiful day, it let them all drop at once.

I call it "Doyle's Tree" because, no matter where we lived, our farms or homes were always referred to as the first owner's. We bought the "Doyle Farm," so it was still His Tree!

Doyle's Tree

By Marjorie K. Randall

1955 - 1973

I'm glad you're such a stubborn tree
And refuse to drop your leaves
Until the last chillday is gone
And the sunshine warms the breeze.
Other trees face cold winter's blast
Shivering, nude from top to root,
But you - you clutch your leaves like ermine,
Dropping a few leaves to warm your foot,
And, glorying in your colors,
You wait for the wind to die down,
Then, casually, drop your winter's cloak
And blossom out in your summer's gown.
I marvel at your beauty
And wait for the message that you bring,
For I know that you're wisely modest
And you will not disrobe until Spring.

Inspiration For
Mom's Prayer

*Laundry occupied my evenings for
quite a few years.*

Mom's Prayer

By Marjorie K. Randall
November 15, 1964

Oh, Bring me your
Tired, poor
Unmated
Socks
So I can match
Up the
Ones in my
Box.

Inspiration For
I Can't Help It If Jaynie Can't Hear

I think '61 must have been a busy year for
me. I'm glad Steve survived it. On this
particular day - I could see him up the street
- and I called time after time.

When he finally came home,
I asked him if he'd heard me. He said,
"Can I help it if Jaynie can't hear?"

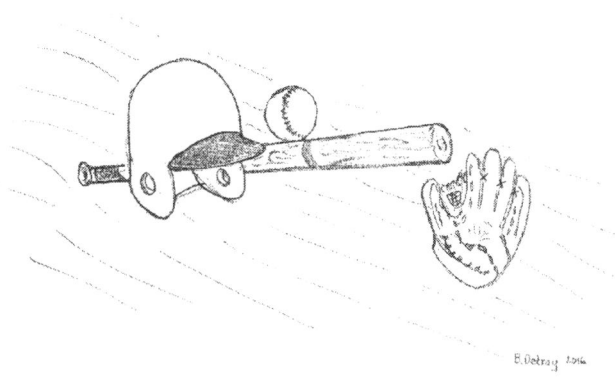

E.Detray 1996

I Can't Help It If Jaynie Can't Hear

By Marjorie K. Randall
March, 1961

Do little boys
Disappear,
At dusk,
To make sure
Their little ears,
At dusk,
Won't hear the call
That stops the ball,
At dusk?

"Put away that bat -
Hang up your hat -
Run upstairs to scour
Dirt saved up for hours!
Sit Down - Not on your knees -
Say your prayers -
Eat your peas!"
At dusk

Inspiration For
Amnesty

*This probably applies to '39, '49', '59,
etc. up to '99. At least, we all keep
on trying to do something for the world.*

Amnesty

By Marjorie K. Randall
March 17, 1969

Freedom! Justice! Equal Rights for Man!
All generations have their fighting plans
To impress upon the world
In which they have matured
To this "peak of man's perfection"
Despite hardships they have endured -
Of unwanted forced feedings
Of health-building preparations
Guaranteed to make them worthy
To sire the Space-Age Generation -
A responsibility so profound
That the mere thought comes steeped
in drugs;
Buried in decibels of instrumentals;
Brewed in potions of exotic bugs.
It's hidden in myriads of colors,
Styles plagiarized from the past,
But flagrantly calculated to prick
Parental conformity to comfort and caste.
Today's young people fight to the Nth degree,
But, shrewdly, reserve the right to beg for
Amnesty!

Inspiration For
Baby Bomb

Lin's daughter, Lisa, at nine months of age!

When I'd put Lisa in her playpen, she'd hang her head over the side and look at the floor and cry. The tears would stream to the floor like a waterfall!

Baby Bomb

By Marjorie K. Randall

1965

I hate to dry
That baby tear -
It's birth was
So dramatic.

Whenever you
Don't get your way -
The explosion
Is climactic!!

Inspiration For
For Sergeant McKieley

I wrote this to Sgt. McKieley when I worked as a mail clerk at the Personnel Confinement Facility my first year at Fort Knox.

Our building was a two-story Army Barracks Building. He used to put tape on the thermostat so that we couldn't change the setting.

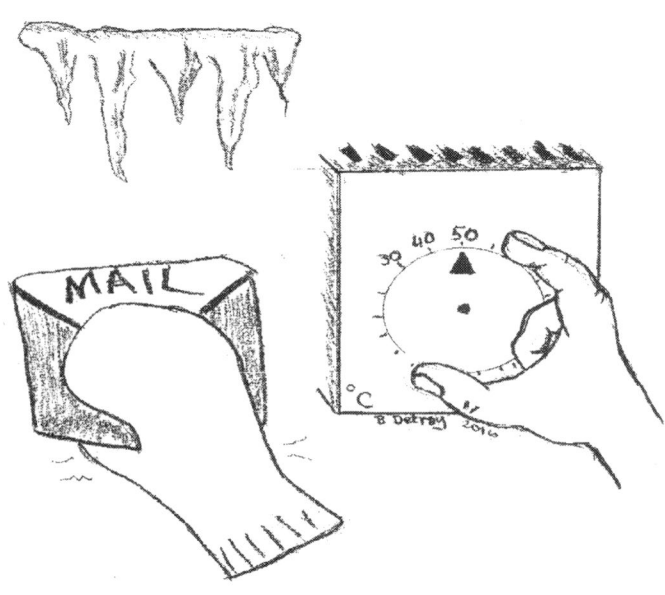

For Sergeant McKieley

By *Marjorie K. Randall*

Deedle, deedle dumpling,
My son John
Wrote up the certified
With his leather gloves on,
Swathed in his coat,
Boots, hat, and shawl,
Because the PFC furnace
Doesn't reach the mailroom
At All!

Inspiration For
The Child So Gold

Barb.

How would a child know that the voices that she heard were not speaking to the rest of the world?

When she was 23, Barb told me of an incident that happened when she was about 3 years old. An Angel helped her floating down the stairs at our farmhouse in Indiana. She described the stairway, narrow and steep, with a small landing near the bottom, with a small window above it, and the remaining steps turning down into the dining room - which had a door that had to be opened. She said that her feet never touched the floor.

Her description of the stairway was so accurate - I had almost forgotten it! We had a difficult time accepting that her illness was real, and several doctors had told me that it was probably coming on for years, and we couldn't recognize it until it exploded into our lives in her late teens.

Comment from Jayne: Barb was diagnosed with schizophrenia when she was a young adult. She struggled with these issues most of her life until she passed away in 2014.

The Child So Gold

By Marjorie K. Randall

July 18, 1973

The child so gold and soft and warm,
Entrusted her Being to the stranger's care
And lifted up her feet and floated down
That steep and twisting stair.

She felt no fright, so didn't cry out,
She smiled and wafted down -
The Angel's hand, high upon her back
Caressing her golden crown.

The child so pure and trusting,
Made the Angel smile
And ask her Lord to please wait,
Just for a little while.

The Angel watched her for many years,
As she romped about and played,
And she spoke to her often in the fields -
The child was not afraid.

She thought the voice was heard by all
The world, and she had no need to see
The form of the friend who spoke to her
Each day as she ran so free.

Throughout the years the friendship grew -
Even the Angel was not aware
That her voice was replacing reality -
The child listened for her everywhere.

continued..

The Child So Gold
(continued)

When the Angel left for a little while,
The child was almost grown -
A young woman, now, prepared to lead
A lifetime, complete, of her own.

The young lass went forth
And tried her best to cope
With the world so harsh, it disillusioned her,
And she began to grope

For the voice of peace and joyous years
With the wind and the open fields
When she had no fears or loneliness,
Nor the burdens Life would later yield.

Tho' she lives at two plus twenty,
My Golden Baby "died" at two,
When her Angel-friend interceded,
For the woman had much yet to do.

The young woman queries such suffering -
Why endure such misery?
But her life has a task yet to fulfill
Before the Angel can set her free.

God's Angel told her many things
That she must express in words
So that others, alone, as she once lived,
Can learn all the truths she heard.

continued..

The Child So Gold
(continued)

So, write your poems, my Golden Child,
The Angel gave them all to you
So you could relay them all to the world -
Words of God - Love - Hope - All true!

Inspiration For
Postcard To Kristy

Aunt Barbie's daughter, Kristy!

Aunt Barbie was having a time keeping Kristy quiet as she recovered, so I sent her this postcard.

Postcard To Kristy

By Marjorie K. Randall
September 14, 1966

Dear Kristy,

Little girls who hop and
Jump and
Leap
On their beds when
Told to
Keep
Still as a mouse should
Just be
Glad
Vitamins and pills are
Not Too-oo-oo
Bad
And make you well e-
nough real
soon
To bounce from your bed
Clear round
The moon!

Aunt Margie

Inspiration For
If You Step On An Ant
It Will Rain!

Aunt Jaynie's daughter, DeeDee!

P.S. Forgive me, DeeDee, but "go" rhymes with "so".

*P.P.S. This year (1997) it rained even harder than DeeDee's rain, and flooded most of Louisville.
So we can't blame DeeDee this time!*

If You Step On An Ant
It Will Rain!

By Marjorie K. Randall
July, 1996

To DeeDee,

The day that DeeDee stepped on an ant
And the rain began to pour -
It came from different directions
Than it had ever rained before.

The rain came in around the windows -
It entered all sorts of places -
It sneaked in underneath the doors -
And flooded all available spaces.

We put towels on the window sills,
Towels all around the doors -
We kept blotting up the puddles
That were "growing" on the floors.

Then, suddenly, the downpour stopped
And the sun came out so bright;
We filled up the washing machine
With soggy laundry that was a sight!

DeeDee laughed and ran out again to play.
She stayed on the porch and we stopped to
watch
An ant crawling by as she jumped
From square to square playing hopscotch.

continued..

If You Step On An Ant
It Will Rain!
(Continued)

Needless to say - another ant died that day
And the sky grew black and electric -
The rain poured around the town
And the storm raged again so hectic!

If you step on an ant, you'll make it rain!
DeeDee proved that this adage is so -
Tho' we had to admit, when she went home,
We were kind of glad to see her go.

Aunt Margie

Inspiration For
A Real Image On An Unreal Mirage

*I've always been fascinated by the mirage
that appears on the long asphalt roads as
you drive in the Midwest.*

*In the distance you can see a mirage that
even reflects the oncoming cars. Someone
behind you can see when your car is
going through the mirage.*

*But you can't see yourself going through the
mirage, so how do you know when you're
in it?*

*Since it's a mirage, there's nothing there. But
if there's nothing there, then how is it
projecting the images?*

*This mystery of a mirage is what inspired
this poem.*

A Real Image On An Unreal Mirage

By Marjorie K. Randall
November 5, 1966

A reflection on a mirage
Is an image wholly unreal
Of something you know exists
On waves you see but cannot feel.

Mirrors you're not sure you've reached-
But, you know that they were there -
Perhaps, now, reproducing you
On that shimmering wavering air.

Only strangers believe a mirage -
You can't watch yourself going through
The elusive, miraculous place
That projects just approaching views.

Inspiration For
To My Husband -
In The Middle Years

*What else can I say. It wasn't all bad,
and you kids were great! And the
grandchildren are such a bonus!!!*

B Detroy 2016

To My Husband -
In The Middle Years

By Marjorie K. Randall

You've left me alone so much that I
Only laugh by myself as life goes by.
I have no one but me to share
The latest news, an idea, a care.
Lately you seem to miss the one, years away,
Who needed only you to love each day.

If we could only go back to when we met,
And trade a moment, life's pattern to set,
I would not be still, no need for words,
Because I loved you so much, you became
        my world.
I would make you talk out loud every day
Even tho' I knew each thought you'd say.

To think love needs only nearness to live as one
Is youth's interpretation, young hope,
        marriage begun.
It isn't until you're older, children grown,
        problems small,
You're shocked to face a stranger,
        suddenly find a wall
Built, unnoticed thru' the years, between two
        who shared
Every moment together in silence - so close –
        hearts bared.

continued..

59

To My Husband -
In The Middle Years
(continued)

What makes this quiet sharing
          now loom as bad,
When it made our marriage so good, life glad?
Perhaps we must start over, a chance to renew
Our beginning oneness, so precious, still true.
Only, now, we must learn to speak our thoughts
To help cover the quiet - children grown –
          laughter naught.

Perhaps now, I need you more
          than you need me,
But, part of our oneness is leaving –
          our children – not we.
We are still together, house quiet, hearts sad,
But, only for a moment,
          'til new routines be had.
Our love we gave our family,
          not needed so much,
We can have back for ourselves, second
          honeymoon, love's touch.

But please don't love in silence,
          this time, speak out,
Because we don't have the children
          to cry – laugh - shout.
I must hear a voice - it's quiet, you see -
Please, put down your paper, and talk to me!
Look this way - discover, tho' I'm gray -
My love waits like a bride on her wedding day!

Inspiration For
This Child

John called to tell me that they had lost a baby, and I felt that its little life should be acknowledged.

This Child

By Marjorie K. Randall
July 28, 1976

For this child our love
Grows nothing but stronger -
We all ache with the wish
That his life had been longer -
Long enough to reach maturity,
From the moment of his birth,
So he'd have his chance to prove
His merit to the earth.
But, what is more proof
Than that this pure little soul
Was plucked by the Lord
Before the bud had reached its goal
Of a life, fulfilled, and bloomed,
With its petals prepared to fall?
When the Lord says, "It's time,"
You rush to heed His call.
The world knows our son's deeds -
The sun shows us he is there
Racing with the winds,
Answering our prayer.
We know him as though he is eighty -
He might have been, you know -
But the Lord said, "Come now,"
And we know he had to go.

Inspiration For
Generation Observation

Beverly!

Beverly made this observation as we passed a cemetery in Kansas when she was 4 to 5 years old. I've laughed many, many times as I recall it over and over.

Generation Observation

By Marjorie K. Randall
June 28, 1997

To Bev,

Is the wind just a great big cloud that blows?
When the rain stops, where in the world
        does it go?
Why does the thunder clap - is it proud
        of the noise it made?
When the sun goes down - does it pull down
        the night like a shade?
Does God have chairs to sit on up in Heaven
        in the Great Blue Sky?
How else could He sit in judgment or answer
        all our "Whys"?
I knew you were my daughter when I heard
        you exclaim,
As we passed the cemetery, and you didn't
        know its name,
"Now, let's see - do you get married or buried
        under rocks?"
What a profound observation from
        my little Goldilocks!

Inspiration For
Redeeming Factors

Steve's son, Michael!

I've always loved Michael's calls.
He tells the truth, good or bad!

Redeeming Factors

By Marjorie K. Randall
October 19, 1995

Michael called and said, "I'm fine" -
"I've been working so hard -
But I got 7 days 'Time-Out'
Because I pooped in the yard."

"Today we pledged the Allegiance
Up on the stage and sang a song -
Then we all got awards -
Now was that so wrong?"

Then Dad got on the phone -
Said, "He didn't tell you all the facts -
He also lied and just finished 'Time-Out'
For some previous bad acts."

Now, last summer, before he was five,
They told me he stood straight and tall
And named the Books in the Bible -
And he really got them all!

They've got to admit -
Michael's not just a "bad" actor -
Sometimes he's a good little boy
With lots of "redeeming good factors!"

Inspiration For
Sunrise Parade

*Muldraugh Hill was on the commute I made
To my job at Fort Knox. I made this trip for
13 1/2 years - but I loved it!*

B Detroy 2016

Sunrise Parade

By Marjorie K. Randall

Daylight brightens on Muldraugh Hill,
The sun accents the trees and the rocks;
The pond reaches up fingers of steam,
The crows call out warnings to the flocks;
The cars creep along with
        their brake lights aglow
When the M-P's white gloves signal "Stop"!

The tanks rumble by on the way to the field
And the traffic resumes at a crawl.
The crows skim across to a
        more appetizing tree
And the M-P's white gloves signal "Stop"!
The sun beams right into your view
You move over the hill - the sky is so blue.

The road curves to the south –
        you move into your lane -
Glad it's daylight so you can
        read all the signs -
You're past the gate where the M-P's wait -
The traffic smooths out - you won't be late -
You approach another light - oh - oh - wait -
The M-P's White Gloves signal "Stop"!

Inspiration For
Postcard To Jennifer

John's daughter, Jennifer!

*It must have been a beautiful
spring that year.*

Postcard To Jennifer

By Marjorie K. Randall

Dear Jennifer,

> Did you see
>> The trees get leaves,
>> The grass turn green,
>> The sun come up
>> This morning?
>
> Did you hear
>> The rooster crow,
>> The tractor go,
>> The buzzing bees
>> A swarming?
>
> Did you feel
>> The fresh warm air
>> Blowing thru' your hair
>> As you danced about
>> So charming?

> Love,
> Grandma

P.S. Have you seen Spring?

Inspiration For
I Am Sure

I have always believed in God.

I Am Sure

By Marjorie K. Randall

Whatever it is
Gives life to the tree,
Gives life to my pet,
Breathes life into me;
Makes raindrops or snow,
Colors each man's skin,
Paints rainbows and flowers,
Bids spring leaves begin;
Divides day and night
Into reasonable hours
By turning the earth
In place with the stars;
Makes birds want to sing
And soar thru' the air,
Makes animals save
Their young in the lair;
Put fish in the sea,
Housed man on the ground,
Then blessed man with will
To find his way 'round
His world.

Inspiration For
The Final Flight

Aunt Jaynie's son, Bradley.

*This was written about Bradley Russell Huth
who died of cancer on February 20, 1996.
His middle name, Russell,
was to remember his grandfather,
Russell Oliver Shuman, who
died on February 20, 1947.*

*This poem was printed with a
picture of Brad for his funeral. The picture
was of Brad in one of his last requests, to ride
in a dirigible. It showed him sitting in the
driver's seat of a blimp, pretending to drive.*

The Final Flight

By Marjorie K. Randall

April 24, 1995

A miracle will never happen
If we give up before it appears.
We can't lose hope as we wait the day
That God shows us why we are here.

We forget, in the throes of pain,
That He's always the One Who cares.
He holds our hands and walks with us
When Life's tests seem
        more than we can bear.

He is the One Who has the plan,
And we must not question "Why?"
He uses our strength and replenishes us
Until we've earned the "Right To Fly."

Inspiration For
Tara Marie

This was about Aunt Barbie and Uncle Derwin's little premature grandchild.

B Delray 2016

Tara Marie

By Marjorie K. Randall
August 20, 1993

You were here such a short time -
Just a little while -
God sent you to enrich us -
To make our lives a smile.

We'll treasure every moment
We got to hold you near,
To share your Precious Beauty,
To love you without fear.

Thank You, Little Angel,
We so wish you could stay -
But you have a Blessed Journey
And you've brightened up our day.

We'll look for you forever
Up in Heaven among the stars -
We'll see the Brightest Twinkle
And know that You were Ours.

Inspiration For
Love On A Bus

Aunt Jaynie and Uncle Gus!

This poem was written at 1:45AM while senile Big Sister was undergoing an ampicillan drip.

Aunt Jaynie had asked me if I could write her a poem about "Take the ring and we'll decide later." Actually, this poem is my true memory of Jaynie and Gus.

Aunt Jaynie and Uncle Gus circa 2002

Love On A Bus

By Marjorie K. Randall
December 19, 1996

Little sister rides the school bus
And she's happy to be there.
When the bus stops for Gussie,
Little boy with the wavy blonde hair.

Little children grow up to be teens,
Still ride the same old bus -
Sister's thinking of the moment
When the bus stops for Gus.

Teen-agers begin dating -
Life becomes so much more fun -
Young sister still loves Gussie -
She knows, now, that he's the One!

Young man proposes marriage -
Beautiful sister seeks advice -
Is she old enough for this step?
Of course! She doesn't even think twice!

Big sister says, "I'll tell you
What our mother said to me -
Take the ring and we'll think about it
And decide later, if this should be!"

Well, fifty years have passed
And you and Gus are still a pair -
I'd say. "The ring is yours, now,
And so is Gussie with the silvery hair!"

Inspiration For
A Size Two View

Lin's son, Scott!

This is why grandparents don't mind becoming great-grandparents, etc. Little children have the sweetest enthusiasm and perspective on the world!

A Size Two View

By Marjorie K. Randall
(and Scotty Randall)
March 31, 1973

Grandma - Come here and look
At the birds up in the tree -
A plane's way up in the sky -
Hurry, Grandma - come and see -
There's a paper under that big bush!
Where'd the plane go? - Watch!
The bird's flying across the street -
Come back - Grandma, there's a bug -
Isn't that butterfly sweet?
The paint's peeling off that board -
I dropped my gum on the ground -
And there's a big brown dog -
Look how he's jumping around!
Oh - Oh - I hear the plane -
The sky's so big and blue -
Grandma - It's really fun
Hanging out the window with you!

Inspiration For
A Child's Wish

This is the first real picture all children make. And they really put their little hearts into it!

A Child's Wish

By Marjorie K. Randall
December 5, 1997

I want to give you a rainbow
So that I can make you smile -
I want to give you God's promise
That things will be fine in a little while.

I know I'm just a little child,
But I always feel your pain -
Sometimes it seems like troubles
Keep falling around us like rain!

All I have is my box of crayons
And a big piece of paper that's white -
I'll make a great big half circle
And its colors must be just right!

I'll draw our house and trees
And put in lots of birds and flowers -
I'll think of our happiest times
And sing about the wonderful hours.

I'll dance around my picture -
I'll make the sky real blue -
I'll put in hugs and kisses
And give all of my love to you.

We'll hang it on the refrigerator
With the magnets that look like fruit -
Maybe you'll want to keep it
Because it looks so very cute!

Jayne's Comments For
The Time It Takes

Although Marge did not provide her inspiration for this poem, I think it speaks for itself.

Too many times we get so caught up in our everyday lives that we forget to spend time with our parents, grandparents, or other loved ones who just want to be with us. Those precious moments together can never be re-captured, and yet they become the memories we treasure throughout our lives.

B Detroy 2016

The Time It Takes

By Marjorie K. Randall
November 2, 1995

It makes me very happy
When you call me on the phone -
But, I find that, for the most part,
I spend my time alone.

You never seem to feel that
You need to see my face -
I know you're all so busy,
You just can't find my place.

I'm so proud of the way you work
And care for your families -
I just wish that I could see them
As they grow up so happily.

I wish that, when I open
The front door to see who knocks,
You'd all be there with pets and kids
And we'd have time to ignore the clock.

Inspiration For
Grammaw's Kisses ("Ugh")

Wally's daughter, London!

Grammaw's Kisses ("Ugh")

By Marjorie K. Randall
September 25, 1994

Dear London,

> You can rub them with your sleeve,
> Or blot them with your hand -
> You can duck them or dodge them,
> But she'll catch you if she can!
>
> She'll just give you more kisses -
> So many, you'll never get away -
> Those kisses are meant just for you
> And, where she plants them
>   they will stay!!
>
> You can't even outgrow them,
> You can run as fast as you can go -
> But, Grammaw's kisses
>   stick right to you
> Whether it's summer or there is snow!
>
> They'll last for years and years
> And you'll be glad some day
> That she catches you and kisses you
> And loves you while you play!
>
> Because you're her little Angel -
> Even when you're a little bad -
> She thinks that you're a wonder -
> The best present she ever had!

Jayne's Comments For
The Bridge

Marge contemplated every aspect of life, including
how the family remembers the legacy of our lives we each leave.

The Bridge

By Marjorie K. Randall
November, 1979

Death is a crossing
    that spans your own beginning
And reminds you of the best things
      and the worst things of your life.
It also brings out the humor,
    and, perhaps, dispels the rumors,
And recalls some moments
    of your greatest strife.

The Family gets together,
    some just discuss the weather,
The rest all hug
    and cry such healing tears -
There's so much to remember,
    and so much that's best forgotten -
What you do right now
    sets the tone for later years.

Inspiration For
Doppler Alerts

Wally's daughter, London.

The sight of London, sitting, surrounded
by pillows in the hall closet, and crying her
own little storm of tears, refusing to come
out of the closet until the exact moment,
on the clock, that the TV channels lifted the
alert, while the dogs and I sat close to her, in
the hall, made me wonder what sort of
"mental havoc" are we wreaking on small
children, making them so afraid of storms?

Doppler Alerts

By Marjorie K. Randall
May 26, 1996

We can't distract kids with a story
Because the storm is almost here -
The TV channels keep cutting in
To fill us all with fear.

The Doppler picture is so ominous
It makes the children shake -
Will this make them braver
If they constantly fear the "Quake"?

Every time a Doppler flash cuts in
Children want to jump into the tub.
We cover them with lots of beddings
And try to calm them with a soothing rub.

Do we overdo the weather?
Turbulence fills our time.
Must we know, for hours and hours,
Every move of each storm's line?

Are we over-alerted to dangers?
Must we analyze each and every breath?
Does it make a better world
If we scare ourselves to death?

Inspiration For
Time To Sing

Daddy and my Littlest Sister, Barbie!

I couldn't sleep on this night and kept
remembering our childhood. I always
thought that Daddy's answer
to "Time-Out" in the '20's and '30's was really
clever. He was a plumber
with a giant heart.

Time To Sing

By Marjorie K. Randall
December 19, 1996

Littlest sister got a nickel
Every time she'd sing
"When Your Hair Has Turned To Silver"
And the applause would always ring.

Littlest sister never got a spankin' -
She was always as good as gold -
The older kids were the "Baddies",
But she did what she was told.

She was as cute as a button -
She had the cutest little nose -
They treated her like a doll baby
And took her wherever they'd go.

When we began to get rowdy
Daddy would pick a flower on the rug -
He'd say, "You sit here!"
And then he'd give us each a hug.

Then he'd place Littlest Sister
In her chair with a book,
And he'd pat her golden hair,
Kiss her, and give her a fond look.

We'd serve our "time" like Indians,
Sitting cross-legged on a flower.
He'd wait 'til we were quiet,
And he'd "free" us in less than an hour.

continued..

Time To Sing
(continued)

If Mother went to the movies,
She'd say, "Now, don't put
        your feet on the wall!"
Daddy would sit in his leather rocker
And gather up us all.

Both little sisters would snuggle in his lap -
Brother and I straddled the chair arms -
And Daddy would rock us and sing,
Feet above the register to get warm.

Now, her hair has turned to silver -
She's so busy with hugs
        her grandchildren bring -
They call Littlest Sister, "Gommie"
And she doesn't have time to sing!

Inspiration For Tomorrow

Wally's daughter, London!

When London was little, the first thing she always asked me was, "Is this Tomorrow?"

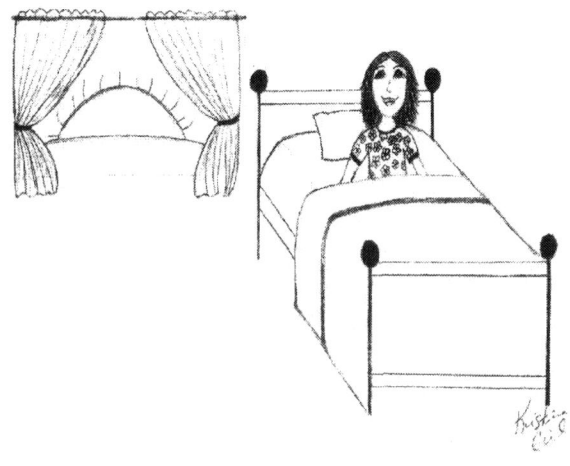

Tomorrow

By Marjorie K. Randall

To London,

When I wake up in the morning
I think, "This must be the day!"
I ask, "Is this Tomorrow?"
But they say, "No, this is Today."

Does it ever get to be Tomorrow?
I search while I'm at play,
But I never seem to catch it -
It's always a day away!

I don't know how Yesterday got here!
I just know, for sure,
It comes when I'm not looking -
It probably sneaks in the front door!

If you want something really bad,
I'll tell you what to say -
Don't ask for it "Tomorrow,"
Just say, "Bring it Yesterday!"

With love,
Gramma

Inspiration For
This Is A Kitchen

My cousin Eleanor!

This is a product of my cousin Eleanor's
comment, "This Is A Kitchen!"

My kitchen is so shabby with the extreme
need for a complete renovation that I always
scheme how to keep everyone in the living
room. Buffet style seems the perfect answer.

But everyone just fills their plate and pulls
up a chair and goes right on
talking in the kitchen!

This Is A Kitchen

By Marjorie K. Randall
June 14, 1997

A kitchen is a feeling -
From the floor up to the ceiling -
That wraps you around the table
While you recall the family fables,
And laugh, and cry, stories from your life,
And exchange solutions for your strife.
Someone always does the dishes
While we discuss our latest wishes,
(The hostess prefers you'll
       get your food and stray
Back to the parlors,
       freshly manicured today.)
But, as we fill our plates,
We pull up chairs to relate
The latest family statistics -
Some pleasant - some more ballistic -
And the cozy glow rises to the ceiling -
The kitchen truly is a feeling!

Inspiration For
Crossing The River

Wally's daughter, London.

*When London comes here, the dogs go crazy –
they bark and jump up and down and bring
their "Doggie Treat" bones into the living
room to chew on. All rules are suspended!*

Crossing The River

By Marjorie K. Randall
July 4, 1997

It isn't easy when your parents are divorced
Sometimes I wish they lived
    two houses down -
Because I'm so tired of crossing the river
To split my week between two towns.

I gather up my violin and my music -
I have books here and books over there.
I can't remember where my ribbons are -
Or my brushes I need to fix my hair.

At least, I always know
    my dogs are at my Dad's -
But, I'm sure they wonder
    what happens to me,
On the days I cross the river, we can play,
And, when I'm gone, they wait so patiently.

Jayne's Comments For
Epic Of A Dewdrop

Only Marge could compose a poem based on the life of a drop of moisture!

B Detroy 2016

Epic Of A Dewdrop

By Marjorie K. Randall
April 14, 1995

The sun takes up a little mist
That it draws up from the sea -
Wind carries it over the land
Until it swirls around a tree.

Night Air cools it down -
It clings to a leaf as it grows
Along with other "mistlets"
Forming a dewdrop hanging low.

It quenches the thirst of insects -
It washes the dust from the leaves -
It mirrors the sun that is rising -
Then it catches the morning breeze.

The breeze carries it back to the Heavens
Where it joins a puffy white cloud
And it waits to become a raindrop
When the thunder claps so loud.

It rains down on the gardens
To make the plants grow tall -
It turns small brooks into rivers
That circle the land until fall.

Winter takes it back to the sky
Where it gets the ultimate chance
To become a beautiful snowflake
And twirl and spin in Life's Dance.

Inspiration For
Upsy - Downsy

Wally's daughter, London!

*London was always practicing gymnastics or
violin or singing, etc. No wonder the house
is so quiet when she's gone!*

*London's birthday is September 25, and she
is now 10 years old! What fun it has been,
watching her grow!*

Upsy - Downsy

By Marjorie K. Randall

1996

Upsy, Downsy - Flipsy Roundsey
Granddaughter's jumping on the bed -
Pictures, shaking, on the wall -
Now, she's standing on her head!

Downsy - Upsy - Hiccsy - Cupsi -
Music, blaring, on the TV -
There she goes, around again -
Faster! Faster! Whee-ee-ee-ee!

Inspiration For
Grandma's Girl

Wally's daughter, London!

Of course, this describes my dear little London!

Grandma's Girl

By Marjorie K. Randall
January, 1995

I smell Bubble Gum, Talcum, and
        "No Tears" Shampoo -
Yes, little granddaughter - I know
        that it is you!
And lots of Puppy Dog's kisses
        all around your ears,
Iodine on your scratches, and
        a few little girl's tears -
Stubbed toes, bruised nose, hangnails,
        tangles in your hair -
Shoes off, clothes on the floor - and
        dear little dollies everywhere!
All these signs mean happiness!
I wouldn't trade you for a Pearl -
To hear you sing and watch you dance -
You give me joy just being Grandma's Girl!

Jayne's Comments For
A Look At Tomorrow

*Marge could always see beyond the darkness
of fall and winter to the beauty of the
coming spring and summer!*

A Look At Tomorrow

By Marjorie K. Randall

It looks like tomorrow
Because everything I see
Thru' dark colored glasses
Becomes magic to me.
The greens are all greener -
Not a trace of parched brown -
The weeds blend right into
The hem of Nature's gown.
The rose looks so fresh
Tho' it will soon lose
Its petals to the wind
Heralding seasonal news -
    "It's bedtime for Nature!
    Set the alarm for next Spring!
    Open the air to Winter sleep,
    Fresh and invigorating!
    Breathe deeply when you arise
    To begin new growing days -
    Live, 'til you're the peak of color -
    Produce your seed - then die away!"
Old things look like yesterday
Because their youth is gone,
But my dark glasses span a year
And preview next Summer's crown!

Inspiration For
My Favorite Sunset

Steve's daughter, Whitney!

*I always love to see the beautiful things the
sun does to her picture on the wall! It seems
to strike the most beautiful patterns in
November.*

My Favorite Sunset

By Marjorie K. Randall

1995

To Whitney,

The November's sun's reflection
Lights your picture on the wall -
Searches out your dimples -
Makes you short - then tall.

It dances on your curls
And flutters across your nose -
It plays across your picture frame,
Studying each little girl pose.

Then, in its last moments
Before it falls down in the West,
It focuses on your pretty smile
Because that's what we both love best!

This is my favorite sunset
Of any time of the year.
It illuminates my Whitney
And almost brings you here!

Inspiration For
Etch-A-Sketch

Steve's son, Michael, drew a picture of
Grandpa Buck
on the Etch-A-Sketch that Christmas while
Buck slept in the chair.

This was another "Michael-Moment" that I'd
love to hold onto and frame and hang upon
my wall!

Etch-A-Sketch

By Marjorie K. Randall
Christmas, 1995

Grandpa napped in the chair,
Specs a-sliding down his nose,
His chin was hanging down
In a sleepy old-man pose.

Michael took the Etch-A-Sketch
And he began to draw
A true portrait of the old-man -
Details of the Grandpa that he saw.

He held the picture up
To show it all around -
Then he gave it a Great Big Shake -
And the image was all gone!

What a sad fleeting thing
Is a child's posterity,
But we saw for a moment,
What an Artist he will be!

Inspiration For
Count Your Blessings

*This was written for all of my children on
the death of their father, Buck.*

Count Your Blessings

By Marjorie K. Randall
January 18, 1997

To my children, and their children, and
    their children's children,
On down the line, indefinitely,
I'd like you to know how proud I am
That you are descended from me.

You've all given my life a purpose -
It was a joy to watch you grow -
You've colored my walls with such beauty -
I just know that I've loved you so.

I never felt the need to join organizations,
Our home was a beehive of activities,
It was fun to guess your futures
With such a variety of proclivities.

We survived wet towels, discarded shoes,
Thirteen pets, boys wrestling on the floor;
Curlers, ironing your hair,
Loud music and friends,
    streaming in the door.

Trivial matters don't really count -
Just always believe in the Powers That Be
And be proud that you belong
To this blessed Family Tree.

Inspiration For
Secret Flags

Comment from Jayne:
This was one of the last poems that Marge wrote. Sadly for us, Marge passed away in 2005. We miss her dearly, but her poetry always reminds us of her love for us.

Probably more than any other, this poem expresses Marge's deep love for her family! She wanted to express this love and remind us that each precious moment of love for our families will become a Secret Flag to encourage us and fill our hearts with great joy!

B DeRoy 2016

Secret Flags

By Marjorie K. Randall
December 28, 2004

If I could tell you all how much I Love you...
My heart would simply burst with
        pride and loving words!
I'd sing a song... a lilting tune!
A most beautiful song...
        the world has ever heard!

I'd paint a picture of all the seasons,
With memories to illustrate...
        each and every one!
You can be sure... I'll take them with me,
When my life on Earth is done!

The total sum of all my life;
Has given me smiles every day!
There's nothing you can't conquer...
If you can just gain a moment, and
        savor it for always!

It's what is inside your heart,
That helps you face the world...
Your own Secret Flags will wave and.
Will always be unfurled!

(To all my Children, and Grandchildren,
Sisters, and Family, who I love with all my
Heart!)

Marge, Jayne, and Beverly 2003

Marge's Legacy

Marge surrounded by Jayne, Wally, Buzz, Steve, and Beverly 2002

Inspiration For
Her Soft Hands

As Marge lay in her hospital bed with her
children, grandchildren, and great-
grandchildren milling about, I noticed for a
brief moment that she was alone. So, I pulled
up a chair and took her hand in mine. I
immediately noticed her hand, only days shy
of turning 83, felt as soft as a newborn baby.

Having never written anything before, I felt
I needed to put this to pen. Looking at this as
a son and a father, I decided to take her
hands back to the beginning and tell the
story of her life.

Steve

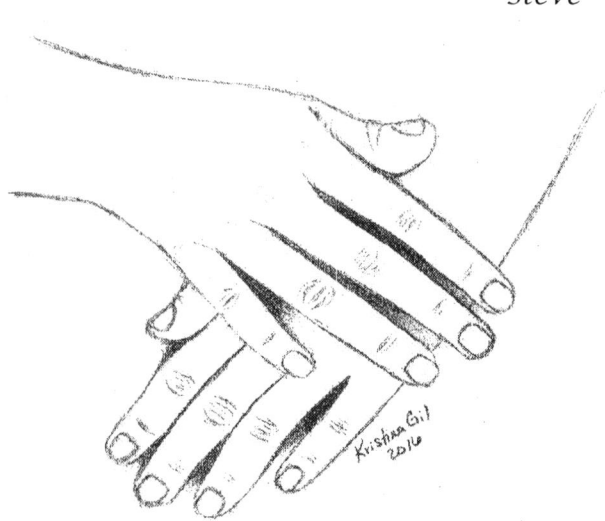

Her Soft Hands

By Steven B. Randall
February 24, 2005

Her soft hands began,
　　The first child born.
So tiny and tender,
　　So fragile, so warm.

Soon came a brother,
　　And one sister, then another.
Those soft hands would play.
　　How they would tease one another.

At home those hands learned
　　To sew, cook, and of gardening.
At school, those same hands
　　Learned of art, and of writing.

Then came a handsome man,
　　So special into her life.
And asked for her soft hands
　　To be his partner, his wife.

Soon her soft hands
　　Had children of her own.
And made every house
　　Into a comfortable home.

From the crack of dawn's light,
　　til the darkness so late,
Her soft hands kept working,
　　To care for their passel of eight.

continued..

Her Soft Hands
(continued)

Those hands took on childhood illnesses,
    And so many scrapes they did mend.
They even pulled one back
    from life's early end.

They held open our doors
    To friends young, and old.
Always to welcome in,
    Not one left out in the cold.

Those soft hands taught us lessons
    In so many ways.
They were my greatest teacher.
    Yes - even today.

Four generations
    These soft hands have touched.
Each one held so softly,
    And loved oh so much.

God watches all,
    From beginning to end.
Her soft hands fell silent
    No more poems to send.

God needed a poet,
    He needed her so.
Her soft hands held mine,
    Not wanting to let go.

continued..

Her Soft Hands
(continued)

Her soft hands now silent,
Her soul it did part.
But her soft hands forever
Touch my soul, and my heart.

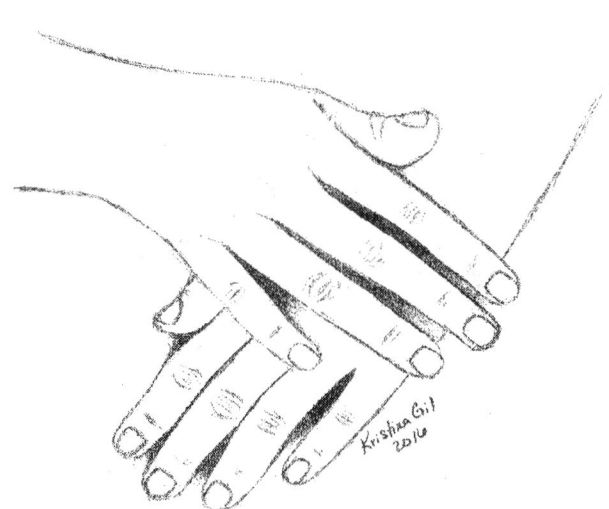

Inspiration For
Epilogue

On Mother's Day, the first since she had passed, I went to visit Marge's grave. I spent a long while tending to her yet unsettled grave, and having a good cry, and talk.

I also had a lot of thoughts and realizations about the day of the funeral. The strongest was how it seemed she had passed along her pen. London, Jaynie, and I had all written poems, each telling a story of their own. The softly falling snow seemed to signal tears of joy for what we had all written.

Steve

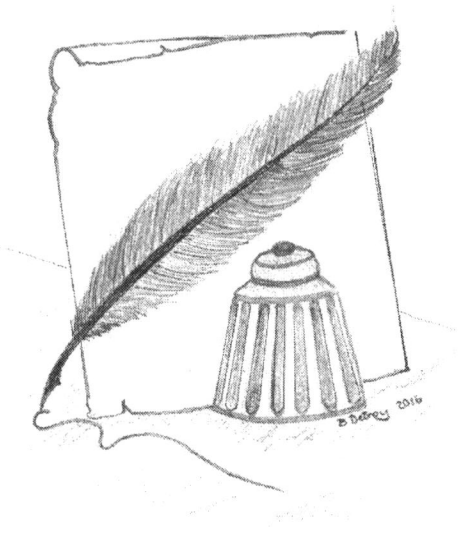

Epilogue

By Steven B. Randall
April 10, 2005

It's been over a month
    Her first birthday not here.
So I went to her grave,
    To talk, and shed tears.

It's such a beautiful spot
    A warm gorgeous spring day.
I listened as the breeze passed
        through the trees
    On the hills far away.

I tended the dirt
    Not settled at last.
I kept some stones for my memory,
    And threw away some found glass.

I'm still trying to understand
    The words that I found.
Flooded with emotions, thoughts,
        and memory,
    I had to write them down.

All of a sudden,
    It dawned upon me.
She had handed me her pen.
    "Son, please write it for me."

continued..

Epilogue
(continued)

She knew I had stories,
    So many things to say.
It was confidence I lacked,
    To say what I could say.

I remember her writing
    All of the time.
She would scribble a verse,
    Then come up with a rhyme.

I now know why she had written
    Things all of the time.
It was her own brand of therapy,
    It brought ease to her mind.

It kept her memories fresh,
    And her thought process sharp.
To write it all down,
    Before it was lost in her mind,
        and her heart.

But it wasn't just me
    Who she had handed the pen.
Children, grandchildren,
    To pass her pen on once again.

A therapy she had chosen
    In her time spent alone.
It widened her heart,
    And let her feelings be known.

continued..

Epilogue
(continued)

Her pen now passed along,
    Does she know we wrote? I say yes.
Here, let me explain,
    In our memory, let us digress.

If you remember the weather
    At the chapel that day.
She shed soft snow tears from Heaven,
    For all the verses read that day.

Inspiration For
Marjorie K. Randall

As we were planning Marge's funeral, the funeral director asked what we would like on the memorial folder. She showed us a binder of examples, but I knew none of them were right for our mother. I wasn't sure what we should use, but I knew that it would be something specifically for Marge.

The next morning I woke at 5:30 AM, and this poem started coming to me. It truly is a description of Marge.

Jayne

A typical picture of Marge crocheting. circa 1981.

Marjorie K. Randall

By Jayne Randall
February 22, 2005

A woman of strength
In body and mind
She stood firm as a rock
And yet she was so kind.

A woman of beauty
With a passion for art
She saw every wondrous detail
Each magnificent part.

A woman of words
Both prose and poetry
She expressed her thoughts and love
To her family.

A woman of love
She gave of her heart
She delighted in her children
A legacy of love she did impart.

Made in the USA
San Bernardino, CA
08 April 2017